★ ALL-TIME ★
BEST ATHLETES

GYMNASTICS SUPERSTARS

ZELDA WAGNER

LERNER PUBLICATIONS ◆ MINNEAPOLIS

Stats in this book are accurate through 2023.

Lerner Publications Company
An imprint of Lerner Publishing Group, Inc.
241 First Avenue North
Minneapolis, MN 55401 USA

For reading levels and more information, look up this title at www.lernerbooks.com.

Main body text set in Mikado.
Typeface provided by HVD Fonts.

Image credits: AP Photo/Amy Sancetta, p. 5; Ed Lacey/Popperfoto/Getty Images, p. 6; Leo Mason/Popperfoto/Getty Images, p. 9; AP Photo, p. 10; Paul Popper/Popperfoto/Getty Images, p. 13; Bettmann/Getty Images, pp. 14, 18; David Madison/Getty Images, p. 17; Toru Hanai/Stringer/Getty Images Sport/Getty Images, p. 21; Laurence Griffiths/Getty Images Sport/Getty Images, p. 22. Design elements: FoxGrafy/Shutterstock; Anna Golant/Shutterstock.
Cover: AP Photo/David G. McIntyre.

Editor: Annie Zheng **Designer:** Kimberly Morales
Lerner team: Martha Kranes

Library of Congress Cataloging-in-Publication Data

Names: Wagner, Zelda, 2000- author.
Title: Gymnastics superstars / Zelda Wagner.
Description: Minneapolis : Lerner Publications, [2024] | Series: Lerner sports rookie. All-time best athletes | Includes bibliographical references and index. | Audience: Ages 5–8 years | Audience: Grades K–1 | Summary: "Gymnastics has had many legends pass through its ranks in its history. Featuring fun stats and impressive feats, readers will count down the top ten greatest gymnasts of all time"— Provided by publisher.
Identifiers: LCCN 2023036868 (print) | LCCN 2023036869 (ebook) | ISBN 9798765625736 (lib. bdg.) | ISBN 9798765628195 (pbk.) | ISBN 9798765632406 (epub)
Subjects: LCSH: Gymnastics—Juvenile literature. | Gymnasts—Rating of—Juvenile literature.
Classification: LCC GV461.3 .W34 2024 (print) | LCC GV461.3 (ebook) | DDC 796.44092/2 [B]—dc23/eng/20230925

LC record available at https://lccn.loc.gov/2023036868
LC ebook record available at https://lccn.loc.gov/2023036869

Manufactured in the United States of America
1-1010185-51907-11/14/2023

TABLE OF CONTENTS

Turn the pages to meet the best gymnasts.
Count them down from 10 to 1.
Number 1 is the best gymnast ever!

MEET THE 10 BEST GYMNASTS!

10. SVETLANA KHORKINA

Svetlana Khorkina was tall for a gymnast.

So she had to be creative with her moves.

COUNT IT!

World medals: 20

9. OLGA KORBUT

Olga Korbut had a fun style on the mat.

She has two moves named after her.

COUNT IT!

Olympic medals: 6

8. NIKOLAI ANDRIANOV

Nikolai Andrianov had a strong body.

He used his strength to do hard moves.

COUNT IT!

Olympic medals: 15

7. SAWAO KATŌ

Sawao Katō was a winner. He won three gold medals at the 1968 Olympics. He won three more at the next Olympics.

COUNT IT!

Olympic medals: 12

6. LARISA LATYNINA

Larisa Latynina was one of the world's best gymnasts. She had the most Olympic medals for 48 years.

COUNT IT!

Olympic medals: 18

5. VĚRA ČÁSLAVSKÁ

Věra Čáslavská competed in three Olympics. She won four gold medals at the 1968 Olympics.

COUNT IT!

Olympic medals: 11

4. VITALY SCHERBO

Vitaly Scherbo won six gold medals in one Olympics. He won four of them on the same day.

janssen/fritsen

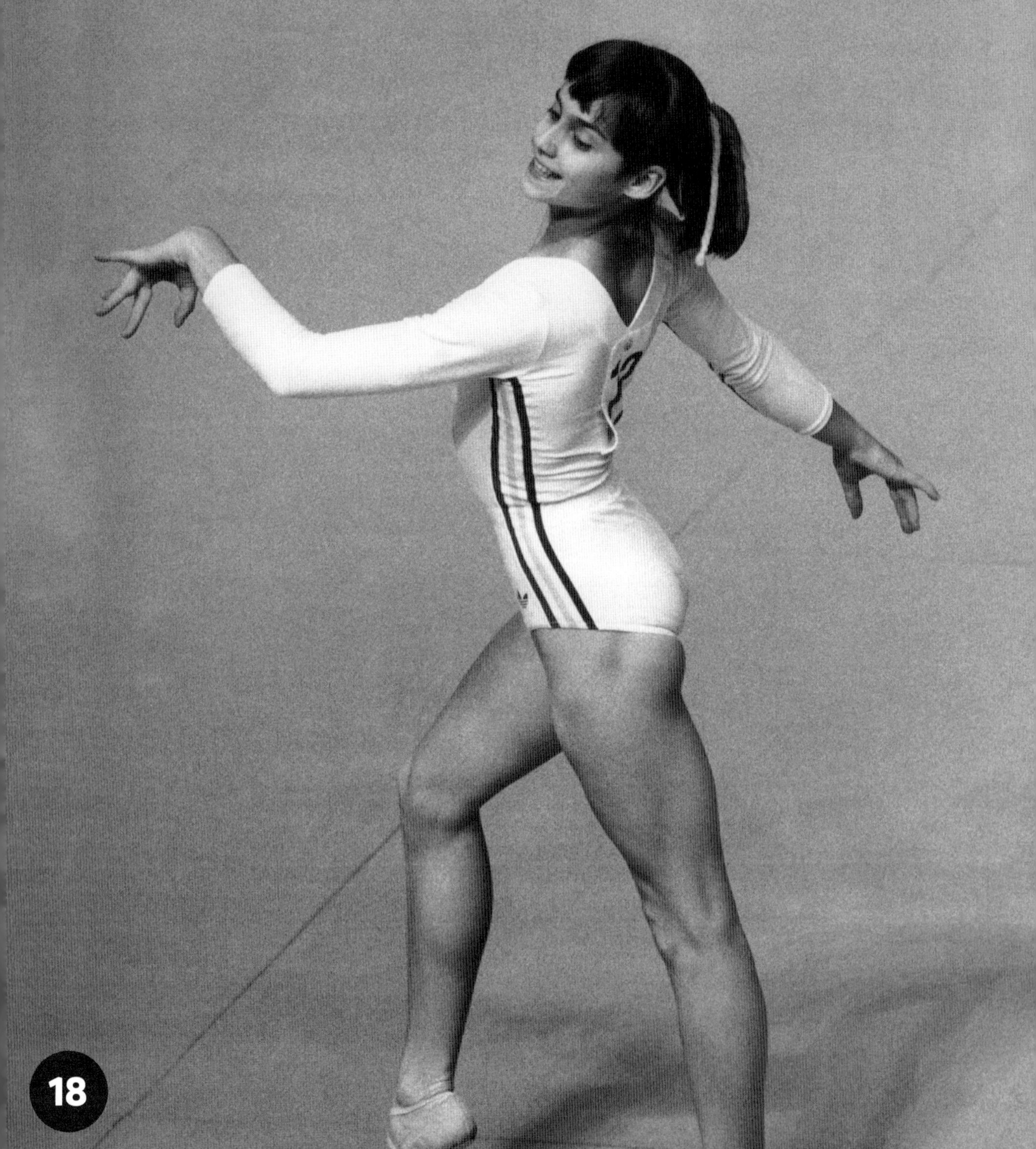

3. NADIA COMANECI

Nadia Comaneci was the first person to ever score a perfect 10. She once scored seven perfect 10s at one meet.

2. KOHEI UCHIMURA

Kohei Uchimura is a gymnastics king. He won every major all-around title from 2009 to 2016.

TableMark
JAL
TableMark
テーブルマーク

1. SIMONE BILES

Simone Biles makes hard moves look easy. Five of them are named after her. She earned the Biles II when she landed it in 2023.

World medals: 30

NOW IT'S YOUR TURN.

Who do you think are the best gymnasts of all time? Make your own list!

GLOSSARY

all-around: when an athlete competes in all the events and is given a score in each event

mat: a soft pad for gymnastics

meet: a large gathering of gymnasts

title: championship

LEARN MORE

Laughlin, Kara L. *Gymnastics*. Parker, CO: Child's World, 2023.

Leed, Percy. *Gymnastics: A First Look*. Minneapolis: Lerner Publications, 2023.

Rose, Rachel. *Simone Biles: Gymnastics Superstar*. Minneapolis: Bearcub Books, 2023.

INDEX

Index

Written by: Ryan Earley
Design by: Savina Magaro
Editor: Kim Thompson
Series Development: James Earley

Photos: Ivan Cholakov: cover; Tony Baggett: p. 5, 9; Rob Crandall: p. 7; Stastny Pavel: p. 11; Jan van der Wolf: p. 13; arrowsmith2: p. 14-15

Library of Congress PCN Data
Garbage Trucks / Ryan Earley
Mighty Trucks
ISBN 978-1-6389-7951-7(hard cover)
ISBN 979-8-8873-5010-3(paperback)
ISBN 979-8-8873-5069-1(EPUB)
ISBN 979-8-8873-5128-5(eBook)
Library of Congress Control Number: 2022942274
Printed in the United States of America.

Seahorse Publishing Company
seahorsepub.com 1-800-387-7650

Published in the United States
Seahorse Publishing
PO Box 771325
Coral Springs, FL 33077

All garbage trucks help!